content

CHAPTER 1: Zoo

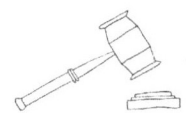
CHAPTER 2: Lawyers 22

CHAPTER 3: Urban myths 46

CHAPTER 4: Life lessons 71

CHAPTER 5: Education 88

Volume 1

Lily Burgess

Illustrations by Dyan Burgess

National Library of Australia Cataloguing-in-Publication entry
Creator: Burgess, Lily, author.
Title: 101 of the best kids' jokes ever. vol. 1 / Lily Burgess; Dyan Burgess.

ISBN: 978-1-925181-89-0 (paperback)
ISBN: 978-1-925181-90-6 (ebook : Kindle)
ISBN: 978-1-925181-91-3 (ebook : epub)

Target Audience: For primary school age.
Subjects: Wit and humor, Juvenile.
Other Creators/Contributors: Burgess, Dyan, illustrator.
Dewey Number: A827.4

© Lily Burgess 2015. This book is copyrighted by Lily Burgess, no part of this publication may be reproduced or transmitted in any form by any means, electronically or mechanically, including photocopy, without permission in writing from the publisher.

When you use single photo/image on social media or for reviewing could you please mention one of our links:
website www.wordsfromdaddysmouth.com.au
instagram @wordsfromdaddysmouth
or twitter @wordsfromdaddys

This is a work of fiction. Any similarity to persons living or dead is merely coincidental.

Published by D & M Fancy Pastry Pty Ltd

Typefaces: Body – Calibri Regular
Titles – Calibri Bold

Important disclaimer
Without limiting the rights under copyright reserved above, no part of this publication may be reproduced, stored, or transmitted in any form or by any means, without prior written permission of both the copyright owner and the above publisher of this book.

The information in this book is of a general nature and is intended to be (at least for some) humorous. It is not intended to be professional advice.

The book is a collection of jokes provided to the author over time and no offence is intended in relation to any aspect of the book.

The author also wishes to convey that this is a book of jokes. It should not be taken out of context and items mentioned should not be tried or actually done. This book is merely for entertainment purposes.

1
Zoo

A cat died and went to heaven. At the gate, he told St Peter how he'd been abused all his life on Earth – people swept him with brooms; he had nowhere to sleep, etc. St Peter tells him he is going to make his life very comfortable in Heaven.

The next day, six mice came to heaven. They gave St Peter a similar story about their hard life on Earth – how they had to run all the time because cats were constantly chasing them.

St Peter tells them he'll make their life comfortable. They ask him to give them skates so that they won't have to do much walking or running anymore. St Peter granted their request and fitted them with skates.

A week later, St Peter was passing by and found the cat comfortably resting. He asked the cat how things were going. The cat says, "Oh wonderful! And those meals on wheels that you've been sending me are delicious!"

A game warden was driving down the road when he came upon a boy carrying a wild turkey under his arm. He stopped and asked the boy, "Hey, mate! Where did you get that turkey?" The boy replied, "What turkey?" The game warden said, "That turkey you're carrying under your arm." The boy looks down and says, "Well, look here! A turkey is roosted under my arm!"

The game warden said, "Now look! You know turkey season is closed, so whatever you do to that turkey, I'm going to do to you. If you break his leg, I'm going to break your leg. If you break his wing, I'll break your arm. Whatever you do to him, I'll do to you. So, what are you going to do with him?"

The little boy said, "Well, I guess I'll just kiss his backside and let him go!"

Late one night, a burglar broke into a house that he thought was empty. He tiptoed through the living room but suddenly froze in his tracks when he heard a loud voice say: "Bob is watching you!" The voice boomed again.

The burglar stopped dead again. He was frightened.
Frantically, he looked all around. In a dark corner, he spotted a bird cage and in the cage was a parrot. He asked the parrot, "Was that you who said Bob is watching me?"
"Yes," said the parrot.

The burglar breathed a sigh of relief. Then he asked the parrot, "What's your name?"

"Clarence," replied the bird.

"That's a dumb name for a parrot," sneered the burglar. "What fool named you Clarence?"

The parrot replied, "The same fool who named the Rottweiler Bob."

One day little Timmy was in his back yard filling in a hole, carefully shovelling earth in and packing it down with his foot.

When he was almost finished, his neighbour decided to investigate.

"What are you doing?" he asks.

"My goldfish died and I've just buried him," replied Timmy.

"That was an awful big hole for a goldfish, wasn't it?" asked the neighbour.

Timmy shot back, "That's because he's inside your cat."

About Sheep and such matters:

Once upon a time a shepherd was tending his sheep at the edge of a country road. A brand new Jeep Grand Cherokee screeches to a halt next to him.

The driver, a young man dressed in a Brioni suit, Cerruti shoes, Ray-Ban glasses, Jovial Swiss wrist watch and a BHS tie gets out and asks the shepherd, "If I guess how many sheep you have, will you give me one of them?"

The shepherd looks at the young man, then looks at the sprawling field of sheep and says, "Okay."

The young man parks the SUV, connects his notebook and wireless modem, and enters a NASA site, scans the ground using his GPS, opens a database and sixty Excel tables filled with algorithms, then prints a 150 page report on his high tech mini printer. He then turns to the shepherd and says, "You have exactly 1,586 sheep here."

The shepherd answers, "That's correct. You can have your sheep."
The young man takes one of the animals and puts it in the back of his vehicle.

The shepherd looks at him and asks, "Now, if I guess your profession, will you pay me back in kind?"

The young man answers, "Sure."

The shepherd says, "You are a consultant."

"Exactly How did you know?" asks the young man.

"Very simple," answers the shepherd.

"First, you came here without being called."

"Second, you charged me a fee to tell me something I already knew."

"Third, you do not understand anything about my business and I'd really like to have my dog back."

A man goes into a cafe and sits down. A waitress comes to take his order, and he asks her, "What's the special of the day?"

"Chilli," she says, "but the gentleman next to you got the last bowl."

The man says he'll just have coffee, and the waitress goes to fetch it.
As the man waited, he noticed the man next to him was eating a full lunch and the bowl of chilli remained uneaten.

"Are you going to eat your chilli?" he asked.

"No, help yourself," replied his neighbour.

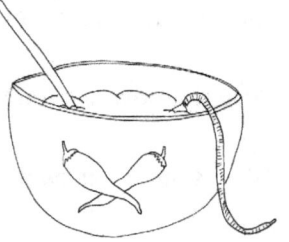

The man picked up a spoon and eagerly began devouring the chilli. When he got halfway through the bowl, he noticed the body of a dead mouse in the bottom of the dish.

Sickened, he puked the chilli he had just eaten back into the bowl.

The man sitting next to him says, "Yeah, that's as far as I got, too."

A polar bear was taking his young baby bear cub out to teach him how to fish.

They went out onto an iceberg, and after a few hours of catching many wonderful salmon, the father polar bear took his cub home, feeling very proud of his son after this wonderful day.

On the way home, the baby polar bear turned to his father and said, "Dad - am I a polar bear?"

His father replied, "Of course you are a polar bear. You have white fur, you catch fish - yes, you're a polar bear."

"Okay," says the baby polar bear.

The next day Dad and baby polar bear go out fishing once again, continuing on with the proud tradition of fish catching, which has been in that family of polar bears for centuries.

Once again, baby polar bear did Dad proud, catching a wonderful Yellow fin tuna.

They were walking home, Dad's arm round his cub's shoulder when once again baby polar bear turned to his father and said, "Dad, am I a polar bear?"

"Of course you are a polar bear. Your fur is white, you catch fish, your mother is a polar bear, and I'm a polar bear. Yes, you are a polar bear!"

"Okay," replies baby polar bear.

The third day, they go fishing, and once again baby polar bear exhibits all the signs that he will one day be a great fisherman amongst the polar bear clan. Dad stands by proudly as baby polar bear catches fish after fish.

They go home, skipping together and whistling, Dad rubbing baby polar bear's head in admiration.

Suddenly, baby polar bear turns around to his Dad and says, (you guessed it), "Dad, are you sure I am a polar bear?"

Dad is starting to get quite angry with this persistent line of questioning.

"Look, you are a polar bear. Your fur is white, you catch fish, your mother is a polar bear, I am a polar bear, your sister is a polar bear, and your grandmother and grandfather are polar bears. There's no doubt that you're a polar bear. Now stop this nonsense."

Baby polar bear is quiet for a while, then turns to his Dad and says, "Then why am I so cold?"

Two vampire bats are hanging up in their cave.

One says to the other, "I'm really hungry. I'm going to get something to eat. Are you coming?"

"No" says the other bat. "I had a big feed last night and I'm still full. You go ahead."

The first bat drops off the roof and flies out through the mouth of the cave.

He's back about 30 seconds later, with fresh blood all over his nose and mouth.

"Wow!" says the other bat, "that was quick! I've never found a meal as fast as that. What happened?"

"You see that big rock just outside the cave?" says the first bat.

"Yep" says the second bat.

"Well, I didn't."

Guy Just Bought A Dead Horse Without Knowing. What He Does Next Is Genius.

A young man named Chuck bought a horse from a farmer for $250. The farmer agreed to deliver the horse the next day.

The next day, the farmer drove up to Chuck's house and said, "Sorry son, but I have some bad news. The horse died."

Chuck replied, "Well, then just give me my money back.

The farmer said, "Can't do that. I went and spent it already." Chuck said, "Okay, then. Just bring me the dead horse."

The farmer asked, "What will you do with him?"

Chuck said, "I'm going to raffle him off."

The farmer said, "You can't raffle off a dead horse!"

Chuck said, "Sure, I can. Watch me! I just won't tell anybody he's dead."

A month later, the farmer met up with Chuck and asked, "What happened with that dead horse?"

Chuck said, "I raffled him off. I sold 500 tickets at five dollars apiece and made a profit of $2,495."

The farmer said, "Didn't anyone complain?"
Chuck said, "Only the guy who won. So I gave him his five dollars back."

Chuck grew up and now works for the government.

A couple drove several miles down a country road not saying a word. An earlier discussion had led to an argument and neither wanted to concede their position.

As they passed a paddock of goats and pigs, the wife sarcastically asked, "Relatives of yours?"
"Yep," the husband replied. "In-laws."

A woman goes to her boyfriend's parents' house for dinner

This is to be her first time meeting the family and she is feeling very nervous.

They all sit down and begin eating a fine meal.

The woman is beginning to feel a little uncomfortable, thanks to her nervousness and the broccoli casserole.

The gas pains are almost making her eyes water.

Left with no other choice, she decides to relieve herself a bit and lets out a dainty little fart.

It wasn't loud, but everyone at the table heard the pot.

Before she even had a chance to be embarrassed, her boyfriend's father looked over at the dog who had been snoozing at the women's feet, and said in a rather stern voice, "Ginger!" The woman thought, 'This is great!' and a big smile came across her face.

A couple of minutes later, she was beginning to feel the pain again.

This time, she didn't even hesitate. She let rip with a much louder and longer fart.
The father again looked at the dog and yelled, "Darn it, Ginger!"

Once again the woman smiled and thought, 'Yes!'

A few minutes later the woman had to let another one rip. This time she didn't even think about it.

She let rip with a fart that rivalled a train whistle blowing.

Again, the father looked at the dog with disgust and yelled, "Darn it, Ginger! Get away from her before she suffocates you!"

Two sea monsters were swimming around in the ocean, looking for something to do. They came up underneath a ship which was hauling potatoes. Seymour, the first sea monster, swam underneath the ship, tipped it over and ate everything on board.

A little while later, they came up to another ship, again hauling potatoes. Seymour again capsizes the ship and eats everything on board.

The third ship they found was also hauling potatoes and Seymour once again capsized it and ate everything.

Finally, his buddy, Heathcliffe asked him, "Why do you keep tipping over those ships full of potatoes and eating everything on board?"

Seymour replied, "I wish I hadn't, but I just can't help myself once I start. Everyone knows you can't eat just one potato ship."

Scientists at NASA have developed a gun designed to launch dead chickens. It is used to shoot a dead chicken at the windshields of airline jets, military jets, and the space shuttle, at each vehicle's maximum travelling velocity – the idea being that it will simulate the frequent incidents of collisions with airborne fowl (bird strike), and therefore determine if the windshields are strong enough.

British engineers, upon hearing of the gun, were eager to test it on the windshields of their new high-speed trains.

However, upon firing the gun, the engineers watched in shock as the chicken shattered the windshield, smashed through the control console, snapped the engineer's backrest in two, and embedded itself into the back wall of the cabin.

Horrified, the engineers sent NASA the results of the experiment, along with the designs of the windshield, and asked the NASA scientists for any suggestions. The NASA scientists sent back a one sentence response:
"THAW THE CHICKEN."

A person who used to work for British Aerospace tells a similar story (which he swears is true) that these machines are actually used to fire chickens into jet engines in order to simulate bird strikes on the compressor blades.

To cut a long story short, someone left the chicken to thaw in the gun overnight, and performed the test in the morning.

The results were somewhat different to those expected and close examination of the high-speed video footage showed a very startled looking stray cat clinging to a half-eaten chicken as it exited the gun at MACH O.7.

David received a parrot for his birthday. The parrot was fully grown with a bad attitude and even worse vocabulary.

Every other word was an expletive. And those that weren't expletives were, to say the least, rude.

David tried hard to change the bird's attitude and was constantly conversing politely with the parrot, playing gentle music; anything he could think of to set a good example.
Nothing worked. Then he yelled at the bird and the bird yelled back. He shook the bird and the bird tried to bite his nose. Finally, in a moment of desperation, David put the parrot in the freezer.

For a few moments he heard the bird squawk and kick and holler. Then suddenly, there was quiet. David was frightened that he might have hurt the bird and quickly opened the freezer door. Not a sound for half a minute.

The parrot calmly stepped out onto David's extended arm and said, "I believe I may have offended you with my rude language and actions. I will endeavour at once to correct my behaviour. I really am truly sorry and beg your forgiveness."

David was astonished at the bird's change in attitude and was about to ask what had caused such a dramatic change when the parrot continued, "May I ask what the chicken did?"

This guy who lived on his own was feeling a little lonely. So he went to the pet shop to find something to keep him company. The pet shop owner suggested an unusual pet – a talking millipede. 'Okay,' thought the man, 'I'll give it a go.' So he bought one and took it home. That night he decided to test out his new pet, so he opened the box and said, "I'm going for a walk. Do you want to come too?"

But there was no reply. He tried again, "Oi, millipede! Want to come for a walk with me?" Again, no response. So the man ranted and raved for a bit, then after a while decided to give it one more try before he took the thing back to the shop. So he took the lid off the box and repeated, "I said I'm going for a walk. Do you want to come?"

"Patience, please! I heard you the first time," snapped the millipede. "I'm just putting my shoes on."

2
Lawyers

The lawyer's son wanted to follow in his father's footsteps, so he went to law school and graduated with honours. Then he went home to join his father's firm.

At the end of his first day at work, he rushed into his father's office and said, "Father, father! In one day I broke the Smith case that you've been working on for so long!"

His father yelled, "You fool! We've been living on the fees from that case for ten years!"

The National Institute of Health (NIH) announced that they were going to start using lawyers instead of rats in their experiments. Naturally, the Lawyers Association was outraged and filed a court injunction. The NIH presented four main reasons for the switch, namely:

1. The lab assistants were becoming very attached to their little rats. This emotional involvement was interfering with the research being conducted. No such attachment could develop with a lawyer.

2. Lawyers breed faster and are in much greater supply.

3. Lawyers are much cheaper to care for and the humanitarian societies won't jump all over you no matter what you're studying.

4. There are some things that even a rat won't do.

Defendant: Judge, I want you to appoint me another lawyer.
Judge: And why is that?

Defendant: Because the Public Defender isn't interested in my case.

Judge (to Public Defender): Do you have any comments on the defendant's motion?

Public Defender: I'm sorry Your Honour. I wasn't listening.

Actual Transcripts from the wonderful world of the Law

Courts:

Q: What is your birth date?

A: July 15th

Q: What year?

A: Every year.

Q: What gear were you in at the moment of impact?

A: Gucci sweats and Reeboks.

Q: This myasthenia gravis – does it affect your memory at all?

A: Yes.

Q: And in what ways does it affect your memory?

A: I forget.

Q: You forget. Can you give us an example of something that you've forgotten?

Q: How old is your son – the one living with you.

A: Thirty-eight or thirty-five; I can't remember which.

Q: How long has he lived with you?

A: Forty-five years.

Q: And where was the location of the accident?
A: Approximately at milepost 499.

Q: And where is milepost 499?

A: Probably between milepost 498 and 500.

As recently reported in the Massachusetts Bar Association Lawyers Journal, the following questions were actually asked of witnesses by attorneys during trials and, in certain cases, the responses given by insightful witnesses:

Q: Now doctor, isn't it true that when a person dies in his sleep, he doesn't know about it until the next morning?

Q: The youngest son, the twenty-year old, how old is he?

Q: Were you present when your picture was taken?

Q: Was it you or your younger brother who was killed in the war?

Q: Did he kill you?

Q: How far apart were the vehicles at the time of the collision?

Q: You were there until the time you left, is that true?

Q: She had three children, right?

A: Yes

Q: How many were boys?

A: None.

Q: Were there any girls?

Q: How was your first marriage terminated?

A: By death.

Q: And by whose death was it terminated?

Q: You say the stairs went down to the basement?

A: Yes.

Q: And these stairs – did they go up also?

Q: Is your appearance here this morning pursuant to a deposition notice which I sent to your attorney?

A: No, this is how I dress when I go to work.

Q: Doctor, how many autopsies have you performed on dead people?

A: All my autopsies are performed on dead people.

Q: All your responses must be oral, okay? Firstly, what school did you go to?

A: Oral

Q: Do you recall the time that you examined the body?

A: The autopsy started at around 8:30 p.m.

Q: And Mr Dennington was dead at the time?

A: No, he was sitting on the table wondering why I was doing an autopsy.

Q: Are you qualified to give a urine sample?

Q: Doctor, before you performed the autopsy, did you check for a pulse?

A: No.

Q: Did you check for blood pressure?

A: No.

Q: Did you check for breathing?

A: No.

Q: So, then it is possible that the patient was alive when you began the autopsy?

A: No.

Q: How can you be so sure, Doctor?

A: Because his brain was sitting on my desk in a jar.

Q: But could the patient have still been alive nevertheless?

A: It is possible that he could have been alive and practicing law somewhere.

AND THE WINNER IS -
Q: Do you know if your daughter has ever been involved in voodoo or the occult?

A: We both do.

Q: Voodoo?

A: We do.

Q: You do?

A: Yes, voodoo.

A lawyer testifying in a case about his performance is asked, "How good are you at what you do?"

His response was, "I am the greatest lawyer in the world."

The judge said, "There is no need to be boastful. Indeed, some modesty would probably help your cause."

The lawyer responded, "Thank you your honour; however, I am under oath."

What's the difference between a good lawyer and a bad lawyer?

A bad lawyer can let a case drag out for several years. A good lawyer can make it last even longer.

A lawyer dies and goes to Heaven.

"There must be some mistake," the lawyer argues.

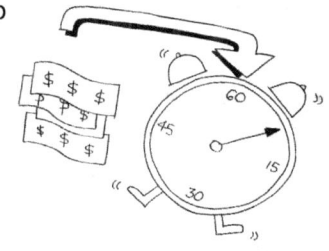

"I'm too young to die. I'm only fifty-five."

"Fifty-five?" says Saint Peter. "No, according to our calculations, you're eighty-two."

"How'd you get that?" the lawyer asks.
Saint Peter replies, "We added up your time sheets."

You have got to love lawyers driven to make the billable hour as profitable as possible.

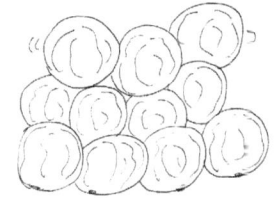

Pythagoras' Theorem: ...24 words

Lord's Prayer: ....66 words

Archimedes' Principle: ....67 words

Ten Commandments: ....179 words

Gettysburg Address: ....286 words

US Declaration of Independence: .... 1,300 words

US Constitution with all 27 Amendments: .... 7,818 words

Legal Regulations on the Sale of
Cabbages in the EU: .... 26,911 words

---

It has come to our attention recently that many of you have been turning in time sheets that specify large amounts of Miscellaneous Unproductive Time (code 5309).

In our firm, unproductive time is not a problem. What is a problem however, is not knowing exactly what you are doing with your unproductive time.

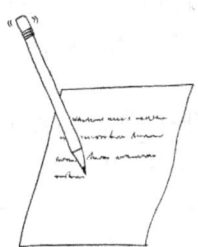

The newly installed Activity Based Costing Financial system requires additional information to achieve its goals.

Attached below is a sheet specifying a tentative extended job code list based on our observations of employee activities. The list will allow you to specify with greater precision what you are doing during your unproductive time. Please begin using this job code list immediately and let us know about any difficulties you may encounter.

Extended Task Code List
Code# Explanation:
1. 5000   Surfing the Net

2. 5001   Reading/Writing Social Email

3.	5002	Sharing Social Email (see codes #5003, #5004)
4.	5003	Collecting Jokes and Other Humorous Material via Email
5.	5004	Forwarding Jokes and Other Humorous Material via Email
6.	5005	Faxing Jokes and Other Humorous Material to Friends not on Email
7.	5316	Meeting
8.	5317	Obstructing Communications at Meeting
9.	5318	Trying to sound knowledgeable while in Meeting
10.	5319	Waiting for Break
11.	5320	Waiting for Lunch
12.	5321	Waiting for End of Day
13.	5322	Vicious Verbal Attacks Directed at Co-worker
14.	5323	Vicious Verbal Attacks Directed at Co-worker while Co-worker Is not present
15.	5393	Covering for Incompetence of Co-worker Friend

16. 5400 Trying to Explain Concept to Co-worker Who Is Not Interested in Learning

17. 5401 Trying to Explain Concept to Co-worker Who is Stupid

18. 5402 Trying to Explain Concept to Co-worker Who Hates you on principle

19. 5481 Buying Snack

20. 5482 Eating Snack

21. 5500 Filling out Time Sheet

22. 5501 Inventing Time Sheet Entries

23. 5502 Waiting for Something to Happen

24. 5504 Sleeping

25. 5510 Feeling Bored

26. 5600 Complaining about Lousy Job (see code #5610)

27. 5601 Complaining about Low Pay (see code #5610)

28. 5602 Complaining about Long Hours (see code #5610)

29. 5603 Complaining about Co-worker (see codes #5322, #5323)

30. 5604 Complaining about Boss (see code #5610)

31. 5605 Complaining about Personal Problems

32. 5610 Searching for a New Job

33. 5640 Miscellaneous Unproductive Complaining

34. 5701 Not Actually Present at Job

35. 5702 Suffering from Eight-Hour Flu

36. 6102 Ordering out

37. 6103 Waiting for Food Delivery to Arrive

38. 6104 Taking it Easy while Digesting Food

39. 6200 Using Company Resources for Personal Profit

40. 6202 Making Excuses after Accidentally Destroying Company Goods

41. 6206 Gossiping

42. 6207 Planning a Social Event

43. 6210 Feeling Sorry for Yourself

44.	6221	Pretending to Work While Boss is Watching
45.	6222	Pretending to Enjoy My Job
46.	6223	Pretending I Like My Co-workers
47.	6224	Pretending I Like Important people When in Reality They Are Fools
48.	6601	Running your Own Business on Company Time (see code #6603)
49.	6602	Miscellaneous Complaining
50.	6603	Writing a Book on Company Time
51.	6604	Planning a Vacation on Company Time
52.	6611	Staring into Space
53.	6612	Staring at Computer Screen
54.	6615	Transcendental Meditation
55.	7281	Extended Trip to the Bathroom (at least 10 min.)
56.	7401	Talking with Plumber on Phone
57.	7402	Talking with Dentist on Phone
58.	7403	Talking with Doctor on Phone

59.	7404	Talking with Masseuse on Phone
60.	7405	Talking with House Painter on Phone
61.	7406	Talking with Personal Therapist on Phone
62.	7419	Talking with Miscellaneous Paid Professional on Phone

---

Lawyer One Liners

Ninety-nine percent of lawyers give the rest a bad name.

You have the right to remain silent. Anything you say will be misquoted and then used against you.

My lawyer told me on the phone yesterday that they had just got lost in thought. Apparently it was unfamiliar territory for them.

There are two kinds of lawyers: those who know the law and those who know the judge.

Mark Twain notes...
"It is interesting to note that criminals have multiplied of late, and so also have lawyers; but, I repeat myself."

I am a lawyer. I can only please one person per day. Today is not your day. Tomorrow is not looking good either.

Like all lawyers I love deadlines.

I especially like the whooshing sound they make as they go flying by.

Never argue with a simple lawyer. They drag you down to their level and then beat you with experience.

Lawyer survival strategy: When you don't know what to do, walk fast and look worried.

Lawyer survival strategy: when confronted by a difficult problem, you can solve it more easily by reducing it to the question, "How would the Lone Ranger handle this?"

Lawyer says client is not that guilty.

Why is it that lawyers call what they do "practice"?

Four surgeons are taking a coffee break.

The first one says, "Accountants are the best to operate on, because when you open them up everything inside them is numbered."

The second surgeon says, "Nah, librarians are the best; everything inside them is in alphabetical order."

Third surgeon says, "Try electricians. Everything inside them is colour-coded."

The fourth one says, "I prefer lawyers. They're heartless, spineless, gutless and their heads and backsides are interchangeable."

Comprehending lawyers
A Lawyer and His Frog

A lawyer was crossing a road one day when a frog called out to him and said, "If you kiss me, I'll turn into a beautiful princess."

He bent over, picked up the frog and put it in his pocket. The frog spoke up again and said, "If you kiss me and turn me back into a beautiful princess, I will stay with you for one week."

The lawyer took the frog out of his pocket, smiled at it and returned it to the pocket.

Frog: "I'll stay with you and do ANYTHING you want."

Again the lawyer took the frog out, smiled at it and put it back into his pocket.

Finally, the frog asked, "What is the matter? I've told you I'm a beautiful princess and that I'll stay with you for a week and do anything you want. Why won't you kiss me?"

The lawyer said, "Look I'm a lawyer. I don't have time for a girlfriend. But a talking frog – now that's cool!"

A man is flying in a hot air balloon and realises he is lost.

He reduces his height and spots a man down below.

He lowers his balloon further and shouts, "Excuse me, can you tell me where I am?"

The man below says, "Yes, you're in a hot air balloon, hovering 30 feet above this field."

"You must be a lawyer," says the balloonist.

"I am," replies the man. "How did you know?"

"Well," says the balloonist, "everything you have told me is technically correct, but it's no use to anyone."

The man below says, "You must work in business."

"I do," replies the balloonist. "But how did you know?"

"Well," says the lawyer, "you don't know where you are, or where you're going, but you expect me to be able to help You're in the same position you were in before we met but now it's my fault."

A woman and her little girl were visiting the grave of the little girl's grandmother. On their way through the cemetery heading back to the car, the little girl asked, "Mummy, do they ever bury two people in the same grave?"

"Of course not, dear," replied the mother. "Why would you think that?"

"The tombstone back there said, "Here lies a lawyer and an honest man."

Position Available Immediately: Articled Sith Lord Apprentice, Dark Side Legal

An unexpected position has opened up in Dark Side Legal for an Articled Sith Lord Apprentice. The ideal candidate for this position would like galactic travel and possess a complete understanding of, and competence with the Force, or demonstrate a willingness to learn.

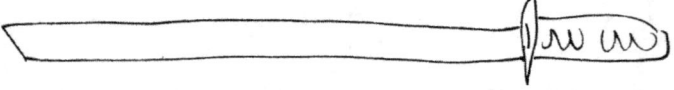

Duties include: Performing competitive intelligence, hands-on intervention in support of the Sith Master's planning initiatives, ability to travel the galaxy widely, and be able to operate a variety of laser-powered hand weapons and high-powered space/air vehicles. Some slaying of enemies of the Dark Side is also required, which may be performed using the Force or hand weapons.

Qualified applicants would need to possess good communication skills (especially when speaking in menacing whispers), and would be action-oriented individuals as weak as risk takers. A background in study of the Force (Light Side or Dark) is desirable, as would typically be acquired by those with advanced degrees, or significant course work in Jedi Arts from the University of Coruscant. Applicants should also be familiar with holographic projection equipment, possess a valid galactic pilot's license (for all classes of ships), and must show a willingness to give in to their hate. A proven track record of using fear and/or Jedi mind tricks to control others is also desirable, as is the ability to speak several galactic languages.

Ideal candidates for this position would also have no children or other living relatives who are strong in the ways of the Force. (A new employee would be given several weeks to meet this requirement.)

Compensation for this position is commensurate with experience, and is extremely competitive for this field of work. Benefits include a generous severance package, a firm starship, and a dark-coloured clothing allowance.

The Articled Sith Lord Apprentice reports to and works closely with the Sith Master, and experience in similar small, team-based organisations is vital to the success of the Master's plans. Discretion is also highly valued, as is the ability to see the future before it happens.

Applications will be accepted until the end of July. Transmit them holographically to: jobs@darkside.com.

A law-firm partner asks a new graduate to think laterally during a client meeting and says, "As an example, if you were to give someone an orange, how would you go about it?"
The young lawyer replied, "Here's an orange."

The partner was livid with the response and said "No! No You have to start thinking like a lawyer!"

The lawyer then recited, "Okay, I'd tell him, 'I hereby give and convey to you all and singular, my estate and interests, rights, title, claim and advantages of and in, said orange, together with all its rind, juice, pulp and seeds, and all rights and advantages with full power to bite, cut, freeze and otherwise eat, the same, or give the same away

with or without the pulp, juice, rind and seeds; anything herein before or hereinafter or in any deed, or deeds, instruments of whatever nature or kind whatsoever to the contrary in anywise notwithstanding…"

A lawyer calls his client to tell him about his fee schedule. "Alright," the lawyer says looking through his papers. "You owe me $1,000 upfront and $417.58 each month for the next thirty-six months."

"What! That sounds like a car-payment schedule," retorted the client.

"You're right. It's mine."

A lawyer named Strange died, and his friend asked the tombstone maker to inscribe on his tombstone, "Here lies Strange, an honest man, and a lawyer."

The inscriber insisted that such an inscription would be confusing as passers-by would tend to think that three men were buried under the stone.

However, he suggested an alternative: He would inscribe, "Here lies a man who was both honest and a lawyer." That way, whenever anyone walked by the tombstone and read it, they would be certain to remark: "That's Strange!"

3
Urban Myths

A man in Alabama died from rattlesnake bites. Big deal you may say, but there's a twist here that makes him a candidate for the Darwin Awards. It seems as though he and a friend were playing catch with a rattlesnake. You can guess what happened from here. The friend (a future Darwin Awards candidate) was hospitalised.

You see, there was a gentleman from Korea who was killed (more or less). He was doing the usual 'walking and talking on his cell phone' when he walked into a tree and managed to somehow break his neck.

Keep that in mind the next time you decide to walk and dial at the same time.

Several years ago, in a west Texas town, employees in a medium-sized warehouse noticed the smell of gas. Sensibly, management evacuated the building, extinguishing all potential sources of ignition including lights, power, etc.

After the building had been evacuated, two technicians from the gas company were dispatched. Upon entering the building, they found they had difficulty navigating in the dark. To their frustration, none of the lights worked.

Witnesses later described the vision of one of the technicians reaching into his pocket, and retrieving an object that resembled a lighter. Upon operation of the lighter-like object, the gas in the warehouse exploded, sending pieces of it up to three miles away. Nothing was found of the technicians, but the lighter was virtually untouched by the explosion. The technician who was suspected of causing the explosion had never been thought of as 'bright' by his peers.

WILL THE REAL NINCOMPOOP PLEASE STAND UP?

AT&T fired President John Walter after nine months, saying he lacked intellectual leadership. He received a $26 million severance package.

Perhaps it's not Walter who's lacking intelligence!

SOME DAYS, IT JUST DOESN'T PAY!

Fire investigators on Maui, Hawaii have determined that the cause of a blaze that destroyed a $127,000 home last month was a 'short' in the homeowner's newly installed fire prevention alarm system. "This is even worse than last year," said the distraught homeowner, "when someone broke in and stole my new security system."

THE GETAWAY

A man walked into a Topeka, Kansas Kwik Shop and asked for all the money in the cash drawer. Apparently, the takings were too small so he tied up the store clerk and worked the counter himself for three hours until police showed up and arrested him.

DID I SAY THAT?

Police in Los Angeles were fortunate with a robbery suspect who just couldn't control himself during a line-up. When detectives asked each man in the line-up to repeat the words, "Give me all your money or I'll shoot," the man shouted, "That's not what I said!"

OUCH, THAT'S SMART

A bank robber in Virginia Beach got a nasty surprise when a dye pack designed to mark stolen money exploded in his Fruit-of-the-Looms. The robber apparently stuffed the loot down the front of his pants as he was running out the door. "He was seen hopping and jumping around with an explosion taking place inside his pants," said police spokesman, Mike Carey. Police have the man's charred trousers in custody.

ARE WE COMMUNICATING?

A man spoke frantically into the phone, "My wife is pregnant and I think the baby is on its way!"

"Is this her first child?" the doctor asked.

"No!" the man shouted, "This is her husband!"

NOT THE SHARPEST KNIFE IN THE DRAWER!

In Modesto, CA, Steven Richard King was arrested for trying to hold up a Bank of America branch without a weapon. King used a thumb and a finger to simulate a gun but unfortunately he failed to keep his hand in his pocket.

In Elyria, Ohio, in October, Martyn Eskins, attempting to clean out cobwebs in his basement, declined to use a broom in favour of a propane torch and caused a fire that burned the first and second floors of his home.

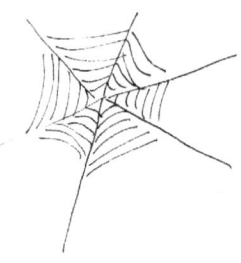

Fire authorities in California found a corpse in a burnt-out section of the forest while assessing the damage done by a forest fire. The deceased male was dressed in a full wetsuit, complete with a tank, flippers, and face mask. A post-mortem examination revealed that the person died not from burns, but from massive internal injuries.

Dental records provided a positive identification. Investigators then set about determining how a fully clad diver ended up in the middle of a forest fire.

It was revealed, that on the day of the fire, the victim went on a diving trip off the coast close to where the forest was situated.

The firefighters, seeking to control the fire as quickly as possible, called in a fleet of helicopters with very large buckets. The buckets were dropped into the ocean for rapid filling, then flown to the forest some 20 miles away from the fire and then emptied.

You guessed it. One minute our diver was making like Flipper Pacific, the next he was doing breaststroke in a fire bucket hurtling through the air. Apparently, he extinguished exactly 5'10" of fire.

Larry Walters of Los Angeles is one of the few people to contend for the Darwin Awards and live to tell the tale. "I have fulfilled my 20-year dream," said Walters, a former truck driver for a company that makes TV commercials. "I'm staying on the ground. I've proven that the thing works."

Larry's boyhood dream was to fly. But fate conspired to keep him from his dream. He joined the Air Force, but his eyesight disqualified him from becoming a pilot. After he was discharged from the military, he sat in his backyard watching jets fly overhead.

He hatched his weather balloon scheme while sitting outside in his 'extremely comfortable' Sears lawn chair He bought forty-five weather balloons from an Army-Navy surplus store, tied them to his tethered lawn chair dubbed 'The Inspiration,' and filled the 4-foot diameter balloons with helium. Then he strapped himself into his lawn chair along with some sandwiches, beer and a pellet gun. He figured he would pop a few of the many balloons when it was time to descend.

Larry's plan was to sever the anchor and lazily float up to a height of about 30 feet above his back yard, where he'd enjoy a few hours of flight before coming back down. But things didn't work out quite as Larry planned.

When his friends cut the cord anchoring the lawn chair to his Jeep, he did not float lazily up to 30 feet. Instead, he shot into the LA sky as if from a cannon, pulled by the lift of 42 balloons holding 33 cubic feet of helium. He did not level off at 100 feet, nor did he level off at 1000 feet. After climbing further and further, he finally levelled off at 16,000 feet.

At that height, he felt he couldn't risk shooting any of the balloons in case he unbalanced the load and found himself in real trouble. So he stayed there drifting, cold and frightened with his beer and sandwiches, for more than fourteen hours. He crossed the corridor of LAX, where Trans World Airlines and Delta Airlines pilots radioed in reports of the strange sight.

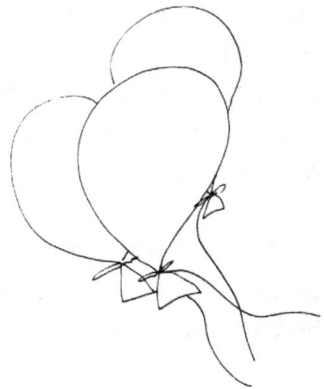

Eventually, he gathered up the nerve to shoot a few balloons and slowly descended. The hanging tethers tangled in a power line, blacking out a Long Beach neighbourhood for twenty minutes. Larry climbed to safety, where he was met by waiting members of the LAPD. As he was led away in handcuffs, a reporter dispatched to cover the daring rescue asked him why he had done it. Larry replied nonchalantly, "A man can't just sit around."

The Federal Aviation Administration was not amused. Safety Inspector Neal Savoy said, "We realise he broke some of the Federal Aviation Act, and as soon as we decide which part it is, a charge will be filed."

Larry's efforts won him a $1,500 FAA fine, a prize from the Bonehead Club of Dallas, the altitude record for gas-filled clustered balloons, and a Darwin Awards Honourable Mention. He gave his aluminium lawn chair to admiring neighbourhood children, abandoned his truck driving job, and went on the lecture circuit. He enjoyed some success as a motivational speaker, but said he never made much money from his innovative flight.

A cop got out of his vehicle and walked towards the kid driving a car who was pulled over for speeding following a speed gun trap. The kid rolled down his window.

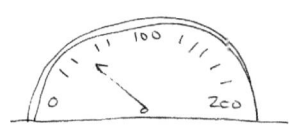

"I've been waiting for you all day, mate," the cop said.

The kid replied, "Yeah, well I got here as fast as I could."

When the cop finally stopped laughing, he sent the kid on his way without a ticket.

I left home in my car last week, heading towards a town about five hours away, when I decided to stop at a comfort station for a 'number two.' The first stall was occupied, so I went into the second one. I was no sooner seated than I heard a voice from the next stall:

"Hi, how are you doing?"

Well, I am not the type to chat with strangers in highway comfort stations, and I really don't know quite what possessed me.

But anyway, I answered – a little embarrassed: "Not bad."

Then the stranger asked, "And what are you up to?" Talk about your dumb question. I was really beginning to think this was too weird! But I said, "Well, just like you, I'm driving east."

Then I heard the stranger sounding very upset, say, "Look, I'll call you back. There's some nincompoop in the next stall answering all the questions I'm asking you."

Do you know the (probably apocryphal) story of the wealthy bank client who told the loan officer he was going abroad for a fortnight and wanted a $5,000 loan?

The bank official said security would be required and the applicant offered his Rolls Royce which was parked outside the bank. All was in order, so the bank official had the vehicle driven to the bank's underground carpark.

When the customer returned from his holiday he returned the $5,000 he had borrowed and the $25 interest. As he handed over the keys of the car the loan officer asked why such a wealthy man would trouble himself with such a transaction.

He replied "Hey mate, I became wealthy by not wasting money. Where else can you find safe covered parking for a month in this city for $25?"

THIRTY-FIVE THINGS PEOPLE HAVE DONE IN AN ELEVATOR

1. When there's only one other person in the elevator, tap them on the shoulder and then pretend it wasn't you.

2. Push the buttons and pretend they give you a shock. Smile, and go back for more.

3. Ask if you can push the button for other people, but push the wrong ones.

4. Call the Psychic Hotline from your cell phone and ask if they know what floor you're on.

5. Hold the doors open and say you're waiting for your friend. After a while, let the doors close, look at an empty space and say, "Hi Greg, how's your day been?"

6. Bring a cat basket and take a nap in the corner.

7. Bounce a ball in the elevator.

8. Drop a pen and wait until someone reaches to help pick it up. Then, scream, "That's mine!"

9. Stand in the corner reading a telephone book, laughing uproariously.

10. Move your desk in to the elevator and whenever someone gets on, ask if they have an appointment.

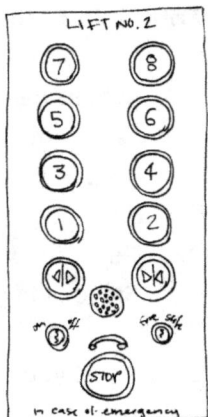

11. When the doors close, use duct tape and work furiously to tape the doors together. Ask for help.

12. Lay down a Twister mat and ask people if they'd like to play.

13. Leave your foot-long python alone in the elevator.

14. Turn off the lights in the elevator to "conserve energy."

15. Ask, "Did you feel that?"

16. Dressed in coveralls, get in a full elevator and when the door closes, push the stop button, post an "out of order" sign inside and go to work on the access panel, saying, "This may take a minute."

17. When the doors close, announce to the others, "It's okay. Don't panic, they open up again."

18. Stand alone, and when the doors open tell people trying to get on that the car is full and that they should wait for the next one.

19. Swat at flies that don't exist.

20. When the doors open, pretend that you bounce off a force field when you try to leave.

21. When people get on, ask for their tickets and check that they meet the "height" requirements.

22. Stand silently and motionless in the corner, facing the wall, without getting off.

23. When the doors close, menacingly announce that, "It's going to be a bumpy ride."

24. Call out, "group hug!" then enforce it.

25. Crack open your briefcase or purse, and while peering inside ask, "Got enough air in there?"

26. Jump rope.

27. When arriving at your floor, grunt and strain to yank the doors open, then act embarrassed when they open by themselves.

28. Greet everyone getting on the elevator with a warm handshake and ask them to call you Admiral.

29. Meow occasionally.

30. Wear a puppet on your hand and use it to talk to the other passengers.

31. Listen to the elevator walls with your stethoscope.

32. Say "Ding" at each floor.

33. Say "I wonder what all these do?" and push all the red buttons.

34. When the elevator is silent, look around and ask, "Is that your beeper?"

35. Draw a little square on the floor with chalk and announce to the other passengers, "This is my personal space."

A man went to the Police Station wishing to speak with the burglar who had broken into his house the night before.

"You'll get your chance in court," said the Desk Sergeant.

"No, no, no!" said the man.

"I want to know how he got into the house without waking my wife. I've been trying to do that for years!"

Long ago, when sailing ships ruled the sea, a captain and his crew were in danger of being boarded by the members of a pirate ship.

As the crew became frantic, the captain bellowed to his First Mate, "Bring me my red shirt!"

The First Mate quickly retrieved the captain's red shirt; the captain put it on and led the crew to battle the pirate ship.

Although some casualties occurred among the crew, the pirates were repelled.

Later that day, the Lookout screamed that there were two pirate vessels about to attack.

The crew cowered in fear, but the captain, calm as ever, bellowed, "Bring me my red shirt!" And once again the battle was on.

This time, the Captain and his crew repelled both pirate ships, although on this occasion more casualties occurred.

Weary from the battles, the men sat around on deck that night recounting the day's occurrences when an ensign looked to the Captain and asked, "Sir, why did you call for your red shirt before going to battle?"

The Captain, giving the ensign a look that only a captain can give exhorted, "If I am wounded in battle, the red shirt will not show the wound, therefore, you men will continue to fight unafraid."

The men sat in silence marvelling at the courage of such a man.

As dawn came the next morning, the Lookout screamed, "More pirate ships are approaching – ten of them, all ready to attack".

The men became silent and looked to the Captain, their leader, for his usual command. The Captain, calm as ever, bellowed, "Bring me my brown pants!"

From the United States comes the following story which reinforces the need to get email addresses correct:

After being almost snowbound for two weeks during the winter, a Seattle man departed for Miami Beach where he was to meet his wife the next day, following the conclusion of her business trip to Minneapolis.

They were looking forward to some warm, pleasant weather and enjoying a break from the children.

Unfortunately, there was a mix-up at the departure gate and the man was informed he would have to travel on a later flight.

He tried to have the decision reversed but was told he had no alternative but to travel on the later flight.

On arrival, he found Miami Beach was having a heat wave and the weather was as uncomfortably hot as Seattle's was cold.
The receptionist gave him a message explaining that the wife would arrive later in the day.

He could hardly wait to get into the pool.

So he hurriedly sent his wife an email message, but because of his haste, made an error in the address.

As a result, his message arrived at the home of an elderly widow, whose preacher husband had been buried the day before.

The grieving widow opened her email, took one look at the monitor, let out an anguished scream and promptly had a heart attack.

When her family found her, the following message was still on the screen:

Dearest Wife,
Departed yesterday, as you know.
Just now checked in.
Was some confusion at the gate.

Appeal was denied.
Received confirmation of your arrival.
Your loving husband

P.S. Things are not as we thought
You will be surprised how hot it is down here.

This is spooky – especially the last one.

You've probably seen this before, but it's still spooooooooooooky! These little 'Jedi mind tricks' are kind of freaky, till you think about them for a little while – then they become more weird. Just follow the instructions below:

DON'T scroll down too fast. Do it slowly and follow the instructions below exactly. Do the math in your head as fast as you can.

It may help to say the answers aloud quietly.

Follow the instructions one at a time, and as QUICKLY as you can!

QUIZ ONE
What is:

2+2?

4+4?

16+16?

Quick! Pick a number between 12 and 5.

Got it?

The number you picked was 7.

Right!!!

Isn't that weird???

QUIZ TWO
Again, as quickly as you can – don't advance until you've completed each of them, really.

Now, ARROW down (but not too fast, you might miss something). What is:

1+5?

2+4?

3+3?

4+2?

5+1?

Now repeat saying the number 6 to yourself as fast as you can for 15 seconds

Then scroll down.

QUICK! Think of a vegetable.

Then scroll down.

Keep going.

You're thinking of a carrot, right?

If not, you're among 2% of the population whose minds are warped enough to think of something else. 98% of people will answer with carrot when given this exercise.

QUIZ THREE
Here is another one. You'll need a pencil and paper for this one.

DON'T CHEAT BY SCROLLING DOWN FIRST!

It only takes 30 seconds. Work this out as you read. Don't read down the bottom until you've worked it out.

a. First, pick the number of days a week you would like to eat out.

b. Multiply this number by 2.

c. Add 5.

d. Multiply this by 50.

e. If you have already had your birthday this year, add 1749. If not, add 1748.

f. Now subtract the digit year that you were born in.

See below:
You should now have a three digit number.
The first digit of this was your original number (i.e. how many times you want to go out to eat each week.)
The second 2 digits are your age.

This is the only year (1999) it will ever work.

Some days it just doesn't pay to get out of bed.
STILL THINK YOU'RE HAVING A BAD DAY? THINK AGAIN.

The following is taken from a Florida newspaper:
It has been reported that a man was carrying out motorcycle repairs on his patio while his wife was in the kitchen inside the house. It is noted that this man was racing the motorcycle engine and somehow the bike slipped into gear. The man, still holding the handlebars was dragged through a glass patio door, and along with the motorcycle, was dumped inside the house.

The wife, hearing the crash, ran into the dining room, and found her husband lying on the floor cut and bleeding, the motorcycle lying next to him and the patio door shattered. The wife ran to the phone and summoned an ambulance.

Because they lived on a fairly large hill, the wife went down several flights of long steps to the street to direct the paramedics to her husband. After the ambulance arrived and transported the husband to hospital, the wife set the motorcycle upright and pushed it outside.

Seeing that gas had spilled on the floor, she fetched some paper towels, blotted the gasoline, then threw the towels in the toilet.

The husband was treated at the hospital and was released to come home.

After arriving home, he looked at the shattered patio door and the damage done to his motorcycle.

He became despondent, went into the bathroom, sat on the toilet and smoked a cigarette. After finishing the cigarette, he flipped it between his legs into the toilet bowl while still seated.

The wife, who was in the kitchen, heard a loud explosion and the husband screaming. She ran into the bathroom and found her husband lying on the floor. His trousers had been blown away and he was suffering burns on the buttocks, the back of his legs and groin. The wife again ran to the phone and called for an ambulance. The same ambulance crew was dispatched and so the wife met them at the stairs once again.

The paramedics loaded the husband on the stretcher and began carrying him to the ambulance. While they were making their way down to the street accompanied by the man's wife, one of the paramedics asked her how the husband had burned himself. She told them and the paramedics started laughing so hard, one of them tipped the stretcher and dumped the husband out. He fell down the remaining steps and broke his arm.

Now, that is a bad day...

Apparently, this bricklayer's accident report was printed in the English equivalent newsletter of the Workers Compensation Board, and is a true story.

Dear Sir,
I am writing in response to your request for additional information in Block #3 of the accident reporting form. I stated 'Poor Planning' as the cause of my accident. You asked for a more detailed explanation and I trust the following details will be sufficient. I am a bricklayer by trade. On the day of the accident, I was working alone on the roof of a new six-story building. When I completed my work, I found I had some bricks left over which, when weighed later, were found to weigh 240 lbs.

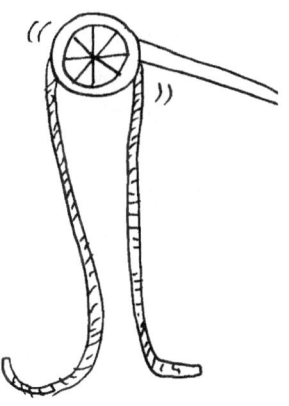

Rather than carry the bricks down by hand, I decided to lower them in a barrel by using a pulley which was attached to the side of the building at the sixth floor level. Securing the rope at ground level, I went up to the roof, swung the barrel out and loaded the bricks into it. Then I went down and untied the rope, holding it tightly to ensure a slow descent of the 240 lbs of bricks. You will note on the accident reporting form that my weight is 135 lbs.

In my surprise at being jerked off the ground so suddenly, I lost my presence of mind and forgot to let go of the rope. Needless to say, I proceeded at a rapid rate up the side of the building. Around the vicinity of the third floor, I met the barrel which was now proceeding downward at an equally alarming speed. This explains the fractured skull, minor abrasions and broken collarbone, as listed in Section 3 of the accident reporting form.

Slowing only slightly, I continued my rapid ascent, not stopping until the fingers of my right hand were two knuckles deep into the pulley which I mentioned in Paragraph 2 of this correspondence. Fortunately by this time, I had regained my presence of mind and was able to hold tightly to the rope, in spite of the excruciating pain I was now beginning to experience. At approximately the same time however, the barrel of bricks hit the ground and the bottom fell out of the barrel.

Now devoid of the weight of the bricks, the barrel weighed approximately 50 lbs. I refer you again to my weight — 135lbs. As you might imagine,

I began a rapid descent down the side of the building. Around the vicinity of the third floor, I met the barrel coming up. This accounts for the two fractured ankles, broken tooth and several lacerations on my legs and lower body. Here my luck began to change slightly.

The encounter with the barrel seemed to slow me enough to lessen my injuries when I then fell into the pile of bricks, and fortunately only three vertebrae were cracked.

I am sorry to report, however, as I lay there on the pile of bricks, in pain, unable to move and watching the empty barrel six stories above me, I again lost my composure and presence of mind and let go of the rope, and I lay there watching the empty barrel begin its journey back down onto me.

Detroit: R.C. Gaitlan, 21, walked up to two patrol officers who were showing their squad car computer equipment to children in a Detroit neighbourhood. When he asked how the system worked, the officer asked him for identification.

Gaitlan gave them his driver's license; they entered it into the computer, and moments later they arrested Gaitlan because information on the screen showed that Gaitlan was wanted for an unsolved two-year-old armed robbery in St. Louis, Missouri.

A motorist gets caught in an automated speed trap that photographs his car. He later receives a $40 ticket in the mail with a photo of his car. Instead of payment, he sends the police department a photograph of $40. A few days later, he gets a letter from the police department with a picture of handcuffs.

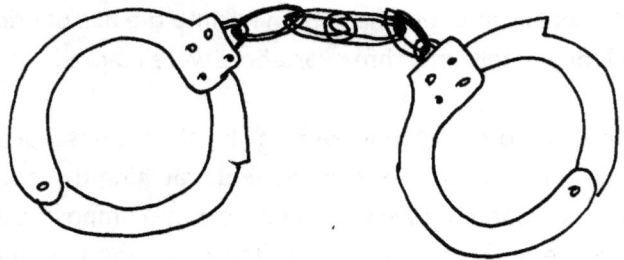

4
Life lessons

1. Never trust a dog to watch your food – Patrick, age 10.

2. When your dad asks you, "Do I look stupid?" don't answer him – Heather, 16.

3. Never tell your mum her diet's not working – Michael, 14.

4. Stay away from prunes – Randy, 9.

5. Never pee on an electric fence – Robert, 13.

6. Don't squat with your spurs on – Moronha, 13.

7. Don't pull your dad's finger when he tells you to – Emily, 10.

8. When your mum is mad at your dad, don't let her brush your hair – Taylia, 11.

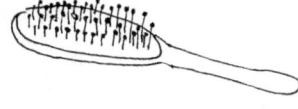

9. Never allow your three-year-old brother in the same room as your school assignment – Traci, 14.

10. Don't sneeze in front of your mum when you're eating crackers – Mitchell, 12.

11. Puppies still have bad breath even after eating a tic tac – Andrew, 9.

12. Never hold a dust buster and a cat at the same time – Kyoyo, 9.

13. You can't hide a piece of broccoli in a glass of milk – Armir, 9.

14. Don't wear polka dot underwear under white shorts – Kellie, 11.

15. If you want a kitten, start out by asking for a horse – Naomi, 15.

16. Felt markers are not good to use as lipstick – Lauren, 9.

17. Don't pick on your sister when she's holding a baseball bat – Joel, 10.

18. When you get a bad grade in school, show it to your mum when she's on the phone – Alyesha, 13.

19. Never try to baptise a cat – Steve, 12.

1950 HOME ECONOMICS: The following information is from an actual 1950s Home Economics textbook intended for High School girls, to teach them how to prepare for married life.

1. Have dinner ready: Plan ahead, even the night before, to have a delicious meal on time. This is a way of letting him know that you have been thinking about him, and are concerned about his needs. Most men are hungry when they come home and the prospects of a good meal are part of the warm welcome needed.

2. Prepare yourself: Take 15 minutes to rest so you will be refreshed when he arrives. Touch up your make-

up, put a ribbon in your hair and be fresh looking. He has just been with a lot of work-weary people. Be a little gay and a little more interesting. His boring day may need a lift.

3. Clear away the clutter. Make one last trip through the main part of the house just before your husband arrives, gathering up school books, toys, paper, etc. Then, run a dust cloth over the tables. Your husband will feel he has reached a haven of rest and order, and it will give you a lift too.

4. Prepare the children: Take a few minutes to wash the children's hands and faces if they are small, comb their hair, and if necessary, change their clothes. They are little treasures and he would like to see them playing the part.

5. Minimise the noise: At the time of his arrival, eliminate all noise from the washer, dryer, dishwasher, or vacuum. Try to encourage the children to be quiet. Be happy to see him. Greet him with a warm smile.

6. Some DON'TS: Don't greet him with problems or complaints. Don't complain if he's late for dinner. Count this as minor compared with what he might have gone through that day.

7. Make him comfortable: Have him lean back in a comfortable chair or suggest he lie down in the bedroom. Have a cool or warm drink ready for him. Arrange his pillow and offer to take off his shoes. Speak in a low, soft, soothing and pleasant voice. Allow him to relax and unwind.

8. Listen to him: You may have a dozen things to tell him, but the moment of his arrival is not the time. Let him talk first.

9. Make the evening his: Never complain if he does not take you out to dinner. Instead, try to understand his world of strain and pressure and his need to be home and relaxing.

10. The Goal: try to make your home a place of peace and order where your husband can relax.

Now, here is the updated version for the modern woman:

1. Have dinner ready: Make reservations ahead of time. If your day becomes too hectic, leave him a voicemail message regarding where you'd like to eat and at what time. This lets him know that your day has been terrible and gives him an opportunity to change your mood.

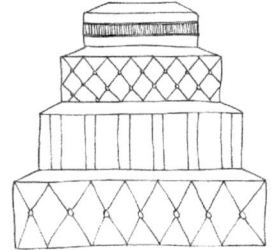

2. Prepare yourself: A quick stop at the cosmetics counter on your way home will do wonders for your outlook, and will keep you from becoming irritated every time he opens his mouth. (Don't forget to use his credit card!)

3. Clear away the clutter: Call the housekeeper and tell her that any miscellaneous items left on the floor by the children can be placed in the Goodwill box in the garage.

4. Prepare the children: Send the children to their rooms to watch television or play Nintendo video games. After all, both of them are from his previous marriages.

5. Minimise the noise: If you happen to be home when he arrives, be in the bathroom with the door locked.

6. Some DON'TS: Don't greet him with problems and complaints. Let him speak first, and then your complaints will get more attention and remain fresh in his mind throughout dinner. Don't complain if he's late for dinner; simply remind him that the leftovers are in the refrigerator and you left the dishes for him to do.

7. Make him comfortable: Tell him where he can find a blanket if he's cold. This will really show you care.

8. Listen to him: But don't ever let him get the last word.

9. Make the evening his: Never complain if he does not take you out to dinner or to other places of entertainment, go with a friend or go shopping (use his credit card).

10. The Goal: Try to keep things amicable without reminding him that he only thinks the world revolves around him. Obviously he's wrong, it revolves around you!

The American businessman was at the pier of a small coastal Mexican village when a small boat with just one fisherman docked. Inside the small boat were several large yellow-fin tuna. The American complimented the Mexican on the quality of his fish and asked how long it took to catch them. The Mexican replied, "Only a little while." The American then asked why didn't he stay out longer and catch more fish. The Mexican said he had enough to support his family's immediate needs.

The American then asked, "But what do you do with the rest of your time?"

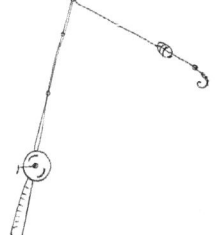

The Mexican fisherman said, "I sleep late, fish a little, play with my children, take siesta with my wife, Maria, stroll into the village each evening where I sip wine and play guitar with my amigos. I have a full and busy life, senor."

The American scoffed, "I am a Harvard MBA and could help you. You should spend more time fishing and with the proceeds, buy a bigger boat. With the proceeds from the bigger boat, you could buy several boats; eventually you would have a fleet of fishing boats. Instead of selling your catch to a middleman, you would sell directly to the processor; eventually opening your own cannery. You would control the product, processing and distribution. You would need to leave this small coastal fishing village and move to Mexico City, then LA and eventually NYC where you will run your expanding enterprise."

The Mexican fisherman asked, "But senor, how long will this all take?"

To which the American replied, "15-20 years."

"But what then, senor?' said the Mexican.

The American laughed and said: "That's the best part. When the time is right you would announce an IPO and sell your company stock to the public and become very rich. You would make millions."

"Millions, senor? Then what?"

The American said, "Then you would retire. Move to a small coastal fishing village where you would sleep late, fish a little, play with your kids, take siesta with your wife, stroll to the village in the evenings where you could sip wine and play guitar with your amigos."

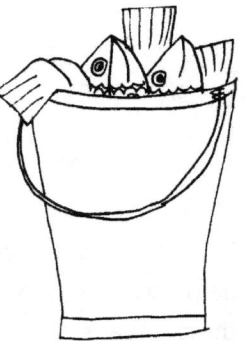

A man placed some flowers on the grave of his dearly departed mother. He started walking back toward his car when his attention was diverted by another man kneeling at a grave. The man seemed to be praying with profound intensity and kept repeating, "Why did you have to die? Why did you have to die?"

The first man approached him and said, "Sir, I don't wish to interfere with your private grief. However, this demonstration of pain is more than I've ever seen before. For whom do you mourn so deeply? A child? A parent?"

The mourner took a moment to collect himself then replied, "My wife's first husband."

FOR SALE BY OWNER

Complete set of Encyclopaedia Britannica.
45 volumes. Excellent condition
$1,000.00 or best offer
No longer needed
Kids know everything

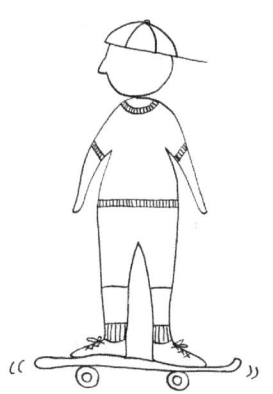

Once upon a time, in a land far away, a beautiful, independent, self-assured princess happened upon a frog as she sat, contemplating ecological issues on the shores of an unpolluted pond in a verdant meadow near her castle.

The frog hopped into the princess' lap and said, "Elegant lady, I was once a handsome prince until an evil witch cast a spell upon me. One kiss from you, however, and I will turn back into the dapper, young prince that I am. And then, my sweet, we can marry and set up house in my castle with my mother, where you can prepare my meals, clean my clothes, bear my children and forever feel grateful and happy doing so."

That night as the princess dined sumptuously on a repast of lightly sautéed frogs legs seasoned in a white wine and onion cream sauce, she chuckled to herself and thought, "I don't think so."

Our David
Which art in Jones
Hallowed be thy Country Road
Thy Cartier watch
Thy Prada bag
In Hermes
As it is in Zambesi
Give us each day our Visa Gold
And forgive us our overdraft
As we forgive those who stop our MasterCard
Lead us not into Katies

And deliver us from Target
For thine is the Chanel, the Gucci and the Versace
For Gautier and Dinnigan
Amex

Dear Mum and Dad,

Our Scout Master told us to write to our parents in case you saw the flood on TV and worried. We are okay. Only one of our tents and two sleeping bags got washed away. Luckily, none of us got drowned because we were all up on the mountain looking for Davey when it happened.

Oh yes, please call Davey's mother and tell her he is okay. He can't write because of the cast. I got to ride in one of the search & rescue jeeps. It was neat. We never would have found him in the dark if it hadn't been for the lightning. Scout Master Chris got mad at Davey for going on a hike alone without telling anyone. Davey said he did tell him, but it was during the fire so he probably didn't hear him.

Did you know that if you put a gas can on a fire, it will blow up? The wet wood still didn't burn, but one of our tents did. Also, some of our clothes got burnt. Dylan is going to look weird until his hair grows back.

We will be home on Saturday if Scout Master Chris gets the car fixed. It wasn't his fault about the wreck. The brakes worked okay when we left.

Scout Master Chris said that with a car that old, you have to expect something to break down; that's probably why he can't get insurance on it. We think it's a neat car. He doesn't care if we get it dirty, and if it's hot, sometimes he lets us ride on the fenders. It gets pretty hot with 10 people in the car. He let us take turns riding in the trailer until the highway patrolman stopped and talked to us.

Scout Master Chris is a neat guy. Don't worry – he is a good driver. In fact, he is teaching Robbie how to drive. But he only lets him drive on the mountain roads where there isn't any traffic. All we ever see up there are logging trucks.

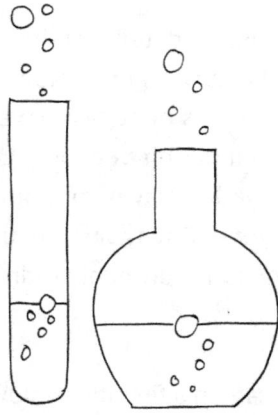

This morning, all of the guys were diving off the rocks and swimming out in the lake. Scout Master Chris wouldn't let me because I can't swim and Davey was afraid he would sink because of his cast. So he let us take the canoe across the lake. It was great. You can still see some of the trees under the water from the flood.

Scout Master Chris isn't grumpy like some scout masters. He didn't even get mad about the life jackets. He has to spend a lot of time working on the car so we are trying not to cause him any trouble. Guess what? We have all passed our First Aid merit badges. When Brad dove into the lake and cut his arm, we got to see how a tourniquet works.

Also, Tyler G. and I threw up, but Scout Master Chris said it was probably just food poisoning from the leftover chicken. He said they got sick that way from the food they ate in prison. I'm so glad he got out and became our scout master. He said he sure figured out how to get things done better while he was doing time.

With love, James.

A lesson in how to be a great flight attendant. Here are some real examples that have been heard or reported:

1. "There may be 50 ways to leave your girlfriend or boyfriend, but there are only four ways out of this aircraft ..."

2. "Your seat cushions can be used for flotation and, in the event of an emergency water landing, please take them with our compliments."

3. "We do feature a smoking section on this flight; if you must smoke, contact a member of the flight crew who will escort you to the wing of the aircraft."

4. "Smoking in the lavatories is prohibited. Any person caught smoking in the lavatories will be asked to leave the plane immediately."

5. Pilot: "Folks, we have reached our cruising altitude now, so I'm going to switch the seat belt sign off. Feel free to move about as you wish, but please stay inside the plane till we land ... It's a bit cold outside, and if you walk on the wings it affects the flight pattern."

6. Pilot, after landing: "Thank you for flying with us. We hope you enjoyed giving us the money as much as we enjoyed taking you for a ride."

7. As we waited just off the runway for another airliner to cross in front of us, some of the passengers began to retrieve luggage from the overhead bins. The head purser announced over the intercom, "This aircraft is equipped with a video surveillance system that monitors the cabin during taxiing. Any passenger leaving their seat before the aircraft comes to a full and complete stop at the gate will be strip-searched as they leave the aircraft."

8. Pilot: "We've reached our cruising altitude now, so I'm turning off the seat belt sign. I'm also switching to auto pilot. This means I can come back there and, for the remainder of the flight, have a nap."

9. The plane landed and was coming to a stop, when a shout came over the loudspeakers: "Whoa, BIG fella ... WHOA ..!"

10. "Should the cabin lose pressure, oxygen masks will drop from the overhead area. Please place the bag

over your own mouth and nose before assisting children. Or adults acting like children!"

11. "As you exit the plane, please make sure to gather all of your belongings. Anything left behind will be distributed evenly among the flight attendants. Please do NOT leave children or spouses!" The purser then continued, "Last one off the plane must clean it."

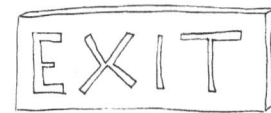

12. And from a captain during his welcome message: "You'll be pleased to know we have some of the best flight attendants in the industry ... Unfortunately, none of them are on this aircraft!"

13. A captain reported that, on a particular flight, he had hammered his ship into the runway really hard. The airline had a policy which required the first officer to stand at the door while the passengers exited, give a smile, and a "Thanks for flying with us." He said that, in light of the terrible landing, he had a difficult time looking passengers in the eye, thinking that someone would have a smart comment. Finally, everyone had departed, except for a little old lady walking with a cane. She said, "Sonny, mind if I ask you a question?" "Why no Ma'am," replied the first officer, "What is it?" The little old lady commented, "Did we land. Or were we shot down?"

14. Overheard during a flight on a particularly windy and bumpy day. During the final approach the

captain was struggling to fight the difficult weather conditions. After an extremely hard landing, a female flight attendant came on the PA and announced, "Ladies and Gentlemen, welcome. Please remain in your seats with your seatbelts fastened while the captain taxis what's left of our aircraft to the gate!"

15. Flight attendant's comment on a less than perfect landing: "We ask you to please remain seated whilst 'Captain Kangaroo' bounces us towards the terminal."

16. After a particularly rough landing during thunderstorms, a flight attendant announced: "Please take care when opening the overhead compartments because, after a landing like that, sure as HELL everything has shifted."

17. From a flight attendant: "Welcome aboard this flight. To operate your seatbelt, insert the metal tab into the buckle, and pull tight. It works just like every other seatbelt, and if you don't know how to operate one, you probably shouldn't be out in public unsupervised. In the event of a sudden loss in cabin pressure, oxygen masks will descend from the ceiling. Stop screaming, grab the mask, and pull it over your face. If you have a small child travelling with you, secure your mask before assisting them with theirs. If you are travelling with two small children, we now suggest you think VERY seriously, and quickly decide which one you love the most."

18. "Weather at our destination is 27 degrees with some broken clouds, but we'll try to have them fixed before we arrive."

19. "Thank you for flying with us and remember. Nobody loves you, or your money, more than us."

20. After a real crusher of a landing, the flight attendant came on with, "Ladies and Gentlemen, please remain in your seats until Captain Crash and the crew have brought the aircraft to a screeching halt up against the gate. And, once the tire smoke has cleared and the warning bells are silenced, we'll open the door and you can pick your way through the wreckage to the terminal."

21. Part of a flight attendant's arrival announcement: "We'd like to thank you folks for flying with us today. And, the next time you get the insane urge to go blasting through the skies in a pressurized metal tube, we hope you'll think of us."

5
Education

JUST IN CASE YOU EVER GET THE TWO MIXED UP

IN PRISON you spend the majority of your time in an 8X10 cell.

AT SCHOOL you spend the majority of your time at a 6X8 desk.

IN PRISON you get three meals a day.

AT SCHOOL you only get a break for one main meal and you have to pay for it.

IN PRISON you get time off for good behaviour.

AT SCHOOL you get rewarded for good behaviour with more work.

IN PRISON the guard locks and unlocks all the doors for you.

AT SCHOOL you must carry around a security card and open all the doors for yourself.

IN PRISON you can watch TV and play games.

AT SCHOOL you get in trouble for watching TV and playing games.

IN PRISON you get your own toilet.

AT SCHOOL you have to share.

IN PRISON all expenses are paid by the taxpayers with no work required.

AT SCHOOL you get to pay all the expenses to go to school.

Dictation Guidelines for Students

Adherence to these guidelines will assure the highest quality transcribed letters in the shortest amount of time.

At the beginning of the dictation, take as deep a breath as you possibly can. Now, try to dictate the entire tape before you have to inhale again.

When dictating a particularly difficult word or phrase, please turn your head and speak directly into your armpit.

We charge per character, including periods. An effective way to cut your cost is to dictate your entire letter as one sentence.

It is not necessary to repeat the same sentence multiple times in the same dictation.

If you have to sneeze or cough suddenly, please remove your head from your armpit and sneeze or cough directly into the microphone.

If you must eat while you dictate, please stay away from foods such as marshmallows, bananas, and pudding. Apples, pretzels, and celery are much better choices.

Please do not stop dictating when you yawn, it throws off our rhythm.

If the client's name is Alan Ratzlaffenhasenphepherzinsky, please have the courtesy to spell "Alan" – there are several possible spellings, you know. For the last name, simply state "the usual spelling".

Do not stop dictating in the event of minor background noise such as a party, the vacuum cleaner, a screaming infant, etc. Again, it throws off our rhythm.

Be sure to place the emphasis on the correct syllable, especially if English is your second language.

Talk as fast as you can. Fair is fair; after all we type as fast as we can.

It is not necessary to repeat the same sentence multiple times in the same dictation.

Please speak as quietly as you can, we want to be able to hear what's going on around you.

If you need to pause for 5 or 10 minutes between words or phrases, pounding the receiver on the desk or repeatedly saying, "still dictating ... still dictating ... still dictating ... still dictating ..." reminds us that indeed, you are still dictating. Just because you need to use the restroom is no reason to stop dictating. Time is money.

Do not dictate so loudly that you disrupt what is going on in the background. In fact, you really should whisper all of your dictation since the information might be confidential.

Similarly, if you are going to watch TV while dictating at home, please watch a war movie with lots of bombing, and be sure to have the volume high enough so everybody in your living room can hear above you talking.

If you need to correct yourself – sorry, correct an error, please do not rewind the tape – sorry, do not back up and record over the error – sorry, wait, the mistake –

just continue with the sentence – wait – go back in the paragraph and fix the error – err, the mistake.

Please go back and just delete that last guideline.

When dictating on your mobile phone from your car, be sure to go through as many tunnels as possible. This will help ensure confidentiality of the information.

(y-o-u) do not need (n-e-e-d) to spell (s-p-e-l-l) obvious words (w-o-r-d-s) for us (u-s). It is our job (j-o-b to know (k-n-o-w) how to (t-o) spell words that (t-h-a-t) we learned (l-e-a-r-n-e-d) in third (t-h-i-r-d) grade (g-r-a-d-e).

Subject: Chinese Proverbs

1. Man who run in front of car get tired.

2. Man who run behind car get exhausted.

3. Man with one chopstick go hungry.

4. Man who eat many prunes get good run for money.

5. War doesn't determine who is right, war determines who is left.

6. Man who drive like hell bound to get there.

7. Man who lives in glass house should change clothes in basement.

Boy: My father's name is LAUGHING and my mother's name is SMILING.

Teacher: You must be kidding?

Boy: No, that's my brother. I'm JOKING. . .

I'm tired because I'm overworked.
The population of this country is 18 million. Four million are retired. That leaves 14 million to do the work.

There are four million who are below the age of five, which leaves 10 million to do the work.

There are three million in school, which leaves seven million to do the work.

Of this, there are three million employed by the Federal Government. This leaves four million to do the work.
One million are in the Armed Forces, which leaves three million to do the work.

One million are unemployed, which leaves two million to do the work.

Take from the total the 1,800,000 people who work for State and Local Government and that leaves 200,000 to do the work.

There are 188,000 in hospitals, so that leaves 12,000 to do the work.

Now, there are 11,998 people in prisons.

That leaves just two people to do the work. You and me.

And you're sitting there stuffing around on email.

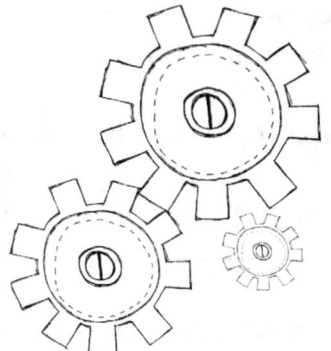

A man goes to the doctor and tells him, "Doctor, that medicine you gave me isn't working. Is there anything else I could try?"

"Fill out this tax form," suggests the doctor.

"How's that going to help me?" asks the man.

"I'm not sure," replies the doctor, "but some of my patients say it gives them relief."

The U.S. Senate is considering a Bill that would tax Botox.

When Botox users heard this, they were horrified. Well, I think they were horrified. It's difficult to tell. – Craig Ferguson

A businessman on his deathbed called his friend and said, "Bill, I want you to promise me that when I die, you will have my remains cremated."

"And what ..." his friend asked, "what do you want me to do with your ashes?"

The businessman said, "Just put them in an envelope and mail them to the Internal Revenue Service. Write on the envelope, 'Now, you have everything.'"

The local bar was so sure that its barman was the strongest man around that they offered a standing $1,000 bet. The barman would squeeze a lemon until all the juice ran into a glass, then hand the lemon to a patron.

Anyone who could squeeze one more drop of juice out would win the money.

Many people had tried over time (weight lifters, oil rig workers, builders' labourers etc.) but nobody could do it. One day a scrawny little man came in, wearing thick glasses and a polyester suit, and said in a tiny, squeaky voice, "I'd like to try the challenge."

After the laughter had died down, the barman said "Okay," grabbed a lemon and squeezed away.

He then handed the wrinkled remains of the rind to the little man.

But the crowd's laughter turned to total silence as the little man clenched his fist around the lemon and six drops fell into the glass.

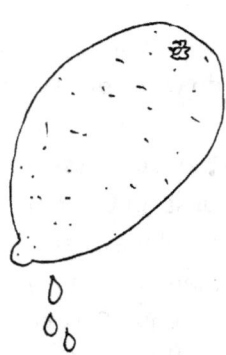

As the silence turned to cheers, the barman handed over the $1,000, and asked the little man, "What do you do for a living? Are you a gym instructor, a weight lifter, or what?"

The man replied, "No, I work for the Tax Office."

The following letter was forwarded by someone who teaches at a small junior high school in Memphis, Tennessee. The letter was sent to the principal's office after the school had sponsored a luncheon for the elderly. This story is a credit to all humankind. Read it, soak it in, and bask in the warm feeling that it leaves you with.

Dear Reyer School,

Thank you dearly for the beautiful radio I won at your recent Senior Citizen's luncheon. I'm 94 years old and live at the Memphis County Home for the Aged.

My family has long since passed away and I rarely have visitors. As a result, I have very limited contact with the outside world. This makes your gift especially welcome. My roommate, Maggie Cook, has had her own radio for as long as I've known her. She listens to it all the time, though with an earplug or with the volume so low I can't hear it.

For some reason, she has never wanted to share it. Last Sunday morning, while listening to her morning gospel programs, she accidentally knocked her radio off its shelf. It smashed into many pieces and caused her to cry. It was so sad. Fortunately, I had my new radio. Knowing this, Maggie asked if she could listen to mine. I told her to get lost. Many thanks to you for your kindness to an old, forgotten lady.

Sincerely, Edna Johnson

Inspirational Quotes for School
1. Do not walk behind me, for I may not lead. Do not walk ahead of me, for I may not follow. Do not walk beside me, either. Please – just leave me alone!

2. The journey of a thousand miles begins with a broken fan belt and a leaky tyre.

3. Don't be irreplaceable. If you can't be replaced, you can't be promoted.

4. Always remember you're unique. Just like everyone else.

5. Never test the depth of the water with both feet.

6. It is far more impressive when others discover your good qualities without your help.

7. Before you criticise someone, you should walk a mile in their shoes. That way, when you criticise them, you're a mile way and you have their shoes.

8. If at first you don't succeed, skydiving is not for you.

9. If you lend someone $20 and never see that person again, it was probably worth it.

10. If you tell the truth, you don't have to remember anything.

11. Some days you are the bug; some days you are the windshield.

12. Good judgment comes from experience, and a lot of that comes from bad judgment.

13. The quickest way to double your money is to fold it in half and put it in your pocket.

14. Timing has an awful lot to do with the outcome of a rain dance.

15. A closed mouth gathers no foot.

16. Duct tape is like the Force. It has a light side and a dark side, and it holds the Universe together.

17. There are two theories about arguing with women. Neither one works.

18. Generally speaking, you aren't learning much when your mouth is moving.

19. Experience is something you don't get until just after you need it.

20. Never miss a good chance to shut up.

21. We are born naked, wet, and hungry. Then things get worse.

SHAKESPEARE RETOLD

Shakespeare: the bard of bards; the greatest playwright who ever lived.
But how many of you have actually read his plays? Fear not, what

follows is a crash course for those who can't be bothered to read them.

WARNING: some of Shakespeare's plays are fairly gruesome and some people like that sort of thing. I have left the gore in as, and where possible.

MACBETH
Witch: Ahhh! That shalt not be hurt until Birnam Woods comes to Dunsinane .

Macbeth: Birnam Woods comes to Dunsinane! Impossible! No one can ever hurt me. Yippee!

Servant: Sire, Birnam Woods has come to Dunsinane!

Macbeth: Oh no . . . . ! [Dies]

END

JULIUS CAESAR
Soothsayer: Beware the Ides of March!

Julius Caesar: Ides of March? That's today! (Gets stabbed, dies]

Soothsayer: Oh no! What have I done? (Stabs himself, dies)

END

A MIDSUMMER NIGHT'S DREAM

Person 1: I love Person 2!

Person 2: I love Person 3!

Person 3: I love Person 4!

Person 4: I love Person 1!

Last person: Help! My head has turned into that of a donkey!

END

HAMLET

A dozen people run on stage and die

END

ROMEO AND JULIET

Romeo: I love you.

Juliet: I love you too

Romeo: I'm going to kill myself.

Juliet: Me too. [Both die)

END

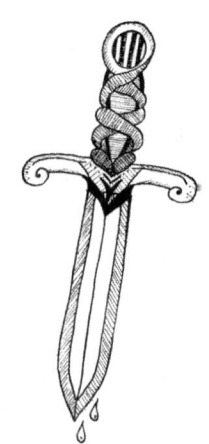

THE HENRIES IN ONE

Commentator: Hello, and welcome to today's American Football game! Today's game is somewhat different than normal, because instead of a ball, the players will be trying to get the Crown of England into the end zone. And oh, wait! They've started! King John has the crown. He's at the 40 yard line, 30. 20 - Oh he's been poisoned! Poisoned on the 20 yard line! Richard I has picked up the Crown. He's started running 20 yards, 30 yards. 40, centre line. He dodges an assassination attempt. But almost fumbles the crown! He's still got it! 40 yards, 30 yards.

He's been shot. Shot by an arrow on the 30 yard line. Henry IV Part One: Wait! He's running back well! 40 yard line! Centre line! Oh, he's been tackled! But that's a superb pass to Henry IV Part Two! Henry IV Part Two is going well! 40 yard line, 30 yard line, 20 yard line! He's going to do it! 10 yard line! He's – oops! He's fumbled. It's been picked up well by his son, Henry, who, if you remember, is on the opposing team!

Running back well towards the centre line, elbowing Falstaff along the way. Oh my! What's this? The Battle of Agincourt has appeared on the field. What's that doing there? Oh my! Henry V has been slain hideously whilst trying to get through the battle! Henry VI Part One has it now. He's looking good for this one! Running well. Past one, past two! He's in the clear! But he's passed it to Henry VI Part Two for no reason.

Henry VI Part Two starts his run. 30 yard line. 10 yard line. Oops! He's been tackled by King Lear.

King Lear makes a break for it. But wait! The referee has blown his whistle! Why has he done that? What? It's a penalty, fictional character on the field.

Henry VI Part Three looks like he's going to take it. He does. Going well ... Oh no! He's been stabbed on the 10 yard line by Richard I.

Richard is going well. He's stabbing anyone who comes at him. Wait! What's this? He's chasing his brother! He's running hard after his brother, waving his sword and carrying the crown! Oh, good tactic! He's employed two other men to stab his brother for him.

Richard II has got on a horse! He's actually riding a horse on the field. 30 yards! 20 yards! 10 yards! Oh, no! The horse is dead! He doesn't like that! But now he's dead as well! Henry VIII has picked up the crown and is over the line! TOUCHDOWN!

Henry VIII has done it! He rightly runs up to all six of his wives for a celebratory hug! What a guy!

Shakespearean Insu t Sheet – very useful for when defeat is snatched from the jaws of victory.

Directions: Combine one word or phrase from each of the columns below and add 'Thou' to the beginning. Make certain thou knowest the meaning of thy strong words, and thou shalt have the perfect insult to fling at the wretched fools of the opposing family.

Hint: Check a Shakespearean Dictionary website for the definitions. Let thyself go. Mix and match to find that perfect barb from the bard!

Column A	Column B	Column C
bawdy	bunch-backed	canker-blossom
brazen	clay-brained	clotpole
churlish	dog-hearted	crutch
distempered	empty-hearted	cutpurse
fitful	evil-eyed	dogfish
gnarling	eye-offending	egg-shell
greasy	fat-kidneyed	gull-catcher
grizzled	heavy-headed	hedge-pig
haughty	horn-mad	hempseed
hideous	ill-breeding	jack-a-nape
jaded	ill-composed	malkin
knavish	ill-nurtured	malignancy
lewd	iron-witted	malt-worm
peevish	lean-witted	manikin
pernicious	lily-livered	minimus
prating	mad-bread	miscreant
purpled	motley-minded	moldwarp
queasy	muddy-mettled	nut-hook
rank	onion-eyed	pantaloon
reeky	pale-hearted	rabbit-sucker

Education

roynish	paper-faced	rampallion
saucy	pinch-spotted	remnant
sottish	raw-boned	rudesby
unmuzzled	rug-headed	ruffian
vacant	rump-fed	scantling
waggish	shag-eared	scullion
wanton	shrill-gorged	snipe
wenching	sour-faced	waterfly
yeasty	white-livered	younker

Insult Hurler: _____
Insult: Thou _____ _____ _____
Definition: You _____ _____ _____

___

They've got to be kidding: those self-improvement manuals, screaming at us from their own special section of every bookshop whenever you go in for a quiet browse about what winning and victory is all about.

They all say the same thing: get up earlier so you can work longer, work out in the gym so you can work harder, plan in detail before starting anything so you can do things better, and exercise ruthless willpower in a relentless pursuit of objectives.

I find this sort of approach totally intimidating and suspect a capitalist plot by a consortium of overpaid chief executive officers to wring even more out of their workers.

I couldn't work this way, could you?

Here is my alternative for the rest of us; a methodology guaranteed to bring victory to anything you might put your hand to – fixing a rickety chair, writing a novel or building an empire without too much exertion.

THE 10 PRINCIPLES OF MUDDLING THROUGH TO VICTORY

(Everyman's not so dynamic guide to success in everything):

1. NEVER PLAN: Planning is a boring, unproductive activity. Scientists have proven that life is too chaotic to plan anything successfully. Trying to make an effective plan is discouraging and an unnecessary waste of time. You may never do what you set out to do if you go down this road; the task will seem impossibly difficult and you'll give up in despair.

2. DREAM: Dreams are far nicer than plans. They can be enjoyed while you stay in bed long after all the planners have gone off to work. Just let fancies drift deliciously into your mind. Be excited by them but don't try to refine them. Let the muddling process take care of the details later. And don't feel guilty – you've started work.

3. WARM TO THE TASK: Take a nice long shower where you can crystallise your dreams enough to contemplate starting. Take your time over this because once that glass door shuts behind you, it's a world of confusion and delusion out there. I suspect that under the shower is the only place to

think constructively; not at the drawing board or staring at a blank computer screen at six in the morning. Enjoy a leisurely breakfast and maybe have a short stroll (none of this power walking). Now you are in the right frame of mind to start.

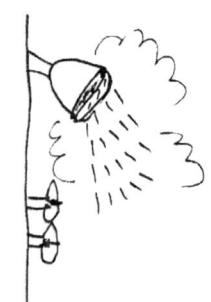

4. BEGIN: Go mindlessly to where you intend to work – at the computer, in the workshop or the garden. The crucial moment has arrived and we don't want to dither about, do we? Muddling is not to be confused with indecision. So, just start. Don't think about where; just do the first thing that comes into your head.

5. RESTART: After a few minutes, it will become clear that you are on the wrong track and you will see where the start should really have been made. This is positive. You can now start all over again, this time with the realisation that you have muddled onto the right track. The process has started working for you. The bit you did before will probably come in useful later anyway.

6. TRIAL AND ERROR: This is the core of the process. Proceed in any haphazard way that suits you. Don't be frightened of going wrong – nothing is wrong without the straitjacket of a plan. Having no preconceived plan gives you the flexibility to go blissfully down any new path.

7. PACE YOURSELF: The secret is a little at a time, frequently. Feel like a break? Take it. Six hours a day is enough for anyone; working longer is unproductive. You'll get lots more done this way than working long hours, and then never coming back to a task that now seems overwhelming. Have an afternoon nap.

8. LIVE WITH CLUTTER: If your desk or workbench gets untidy while you are at work, don't worry, just keep going. Being able to cope with confusion is a sign of superior intelligence. When it's time to do something else for a change, this is the time to sweep up or tidy the desktop – if you really feel like it.

9. THE WAY AHEAD: As the task muddles along, there will come a time when a shape emerges; the way becomes clear in a far more detailed and integrated way than could ever have been planned for. Go for it!

10. I can't think of one. I should never have planned for 10. See what I mean? That'll have to do.

This assignment was actually turned in by two English students: Rebecca (last name deleted) and Gary (last name deleted).

English - A Creative Writing
Prof Miller
In-class Assignment for Wednesday

Today we will experiment with a new form called the tandem story. The process is simple. Each person will pair off with the person sitting to his or her immediate right. One of you will then write the first paragraph of a short story. The partner will read the first paragraph and then add another paragraph to the story. The first person will then add a third paragraph, and so on back and forth. Remember to re-read what has been written each time in order to keep the story coherent. The story is over when both agree a conclusion has been reached.

At first, Laurie couldn't decide which kind of tea she wanted. The camomile, which used to be her favourite for lazy evenings at home, now reminded her too much of Carl, who once said (in happier times) that he liked camomile. But she felt she must now, at all costs, keep her mind off Carl. His possessiveness was suffocating and if she thought about him too much her asthma started acting up again. So camomile was out of the question

Meanwhile, Advance Sergeant Carl Harris, leader of the attack squadron now in orbit over Skylon 4, had more important things to think about than the neuroses of an air-headed asthmatic bimbo named Laurie with whom he had spent one day with over a year ago.

"A.S. Harris to Geostation 17," he said into his trans galactic communicator. "Polar orbit established. No sign of resistance so far ..." But before he could sign off, a bluish particle beam flashed out of nowhere and blasted a hole through his ship's cargo bay. The jolt from the direct hit sent him flying out of his seat and across the cockpit.

He bumped his head and died almost immediately, but not before he felt one last pang of regret for the one woman who had ever had feelings for him. Soon afterwards, Earth stopped its pointless hostilities towards the peaceful farmers of Skylon 4.

"Congress passes law permanently abolishing war and space travel," Laurie reads in her newspaper one morning. The news simultaneously excited her and bored her. She stared out the window, dreaming of her youth, when the days had passed unhurriedly and carefree, with no newspapers to read, no television to distract her from her sense of innocent wonder at all the beautiful things around her. '*Why?*' she pondered wistfully.

Little did she know, but she had less than 10 seconds to live. Thousands of miles above the city, the Anu'udrian mothership launched the first of its lithium fusion missiles. The dim-witted wimpy peaceniks who pushed the Unilateral Aerospace Disarmament Treaty through

Congress had left Earth a defenceless target for the hostile alien empires who were determined to destroy the human race. Within two hours after the passage of the treaty, the Anu'udrian ships were on course for Earth's orbit with enough firepower to pulverise the entire planet. With no one to stop them, they swiftly initiated their diabolical plan and the lithium fusion missile entered the atmosphere unimpeded. The President, in his top secret mobile submarine headquarters on the ocean floor off the coast of Guam, felt the inconceivably massive explosion which vaporised Laurie and 85 million other Americans. The President slammed his fist on the conference table. "We can't allow this! I'm going to veto that treaty! Let's blow them out of the sky!"

This is absurd. I refuse to continue this mockery of literature. My writing partner is a violent, chauvinistic, semi-literate adolescent.

Yeah? Well, you're a self-centred tedious neurotic whose attempts at writing are the literary equivalent of Valium.

WISDOM THAT MOVIES PROVIDE!
THINGS YOU WOULD NEVER KNOW WITHOUT MOVIES

1. Large, loft-style apartments in New York City are well within the price range of most people - whether they are employed or not.

2. One of a pair of identical twins is always born evil.

3. Should you decide to defuse a bomb, don't worry which wire to cut. You will always choose the right one.

4. Most laptop computers are powerful enough to override the communications system of any invading alien society.

5. It does not matter if you are heavily outnumbered in a fight involving martial arts. Your enemies will wait patiently to attack you one by one by dancing around in a threatening manner until you have knocked out their predecessors.

6. When you turn out the light to go to bed, everything in your bedroom will still be clearly visible – just slightly bluish.

7. If you are blonde and pretty, it is possible to become a world expert on nuclear fission at the age of 22.

8. Honest and hardworking policemen are traditionally gunned down three days before their retirement.

9. Rather than wasting bullets, megalomaniacs prefer to kill their archenemies using complicated machinery involving fuses, pulley systems, deadly gasses, lasers, and man-eating sharks, which will allow their captives at least 20 minutes to escape.

10. During all police investigations, it will be necessary to visit a fancy night club with loud music at least once.

11. All grocery shopping bags contain at least one stick of French bread.

12. It's easy for anyone to land a plane providing there is someone in the control tower to talk you down.

13. Once applied, lipstick will never rub off – even while scuba diving.

14. In war, it is impossible to die unless you make the mistake of showing someone a picture of your sweetheart back home.

15. Should you wish to pass yourself off as a German or Russian officer, it will not be necessary to speak the language: a German or Russian accent will do. (It used to be an English accent for the Germans).

16. The Eiffel Tower can be seen from any window in Paris.

17. A man will show no pain while taking the most ferocious beating, but will wince when a woman tries to clean his wounds.

18. If a large pane of glass is visible, someone will be thrown through it before long.

19. Word processors never display a cursor on screen but will always say: Enter password now.

20. Even when driving down a perfectly straight road, it is necessary to turn the steering wheel vigorously from left to right every few moments.

21. All bombs are fitted with electronic timing devices with large red readouts so you know exactly when they're going to go off.

22. A detective can only solve a case once he has been suspended from duty.

23. If you decide to start dancing in the street, everyone you meet will know all the steps.

24. Police departments give their officers personality tests to make sure they are deliberately assigned a partner who is their total opposite.

25. When they are alone, all foreign military officers prefer to speak to each other in English.

An elderly man lay dying in his bed. In death's agony, he suddenly smelled the aroma of his favourite chocolate chip cookies wafting up the stairs. He gathered his remaining strength, and lifted himself from the bed. Leaning against the wall, he slowly made his way out of the bedroom, and with even greater effort forced himself crawling down the stairs gripping the railing with both hands.

With laboured breath, he leaned against the door-frame, gazing into the kitchen.

Were it not for death's agony, he would have thought himself already in heaven. There, spread out on waxed paper on the kitchen table, were literally hundreds of his favourite chocolate chip cookies.

Was it heaven? Or was it one final act of heroic love from his devoted wife, ensuring that he left this world a happy man?

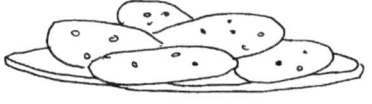

Mustering one great final effort, he threw himself toward the table, landing in a rumpled posture. His parched lips parted: the wondrous taste of the cookie was already in his mouth, seemingly bringing him back to life. The aged and withered hand trembled on its way to a cookie at the edge of the table, when it was suddenly smacked with a spatula by his wife.

"Get out now!" she screamed, "They're for the funeral".

Once there was a guy named Joe. One day he died and found himself standing in front of the Pearly Gates.
St. Peter: "Joe, if you can answer one question, I'll let you into heaven."

Joe: "Sounds easy enough."

St. Peter: "Okay, who is with you always?"

Joe: "Oh, that's easy: Andy!"

St. Peter: "Andy?"

Joe: "Yeah, haven't you heard that hymn, 'Andy walks with me, Andy talks with me?'"

Other books from the Words from Daddy's Mouth Studio

Early Childhood Readers (ages 4 – 6)

Broken Bones
When my dad was little, he had an old yellow bike.
But his friend's bike, which was new, was a red racer.

Find out what happens when dad swaps his bike with his friend in *Broken Bones*.

Radio Competitions
When my dad was little, he liked to listen to the radio.
Sometimes the radio station had competitions.

Find out what happens when dad tries to win a prize in *Radio Competitions*.

The Sports Room
When my dad was little, he used to help look after the school sports room.
Some of his friends helped too.
Find out what happens when dad puts away the sports equipment in *The Sports Room*.

The Ball Game

When my dad was little, he liked to play ball games.

One game, called 'Brandings', was like hide-and-seek.

Find out what happens when dad plays 'Brandings' in *The Ball Game*.

Younger Readers (ages 7 – 10)

Book One
The Big Rusty Nail

The Big Rusty Nail is an entertaining journey of a day in the life of a primary school sports room monitor, shared between a dad and his young children.

The story also provides a modern take on the proverb 'A Stitch in Time Saves Nine.' That is, stopping something before it happens is often better than having to fix things up after the event.

Book Two
The Terrible Red Racer

What happens when Dad swaps his yellow BMX bike for his friend's red racer? Find out in the latest 'Words from Daddy's Mouth'— The Terrible Red Racer. The story also provides a modern take on 'Murphy's Law.' That is, what can go wrong, will go wrong.

Book Three
The Weekend Cash Call

Find out about some of the things that dad has won from radio competitions in the latest book from the 'Words from Daddy's mouth' series - 'The Weekend Cash Call.' The story provides a modern take on the proverb that 'Fortune favours the brave.'

Book Four
The Brandings Game

For Dad, there was something even worse than the Terrible Red Racer and this was 'The Brandings Game' - the latest book in the Words from Daddy's Mouth series.

The story provides a modern take on the proverb 'Look before you leap.'

Chapter Books (ages 7 – 10)

Book Five
The Most Amazing Golf Shot Ever
Golf was another sport that Dad was really good at; or was he? Find out in the latest 'Words from Daddy's Mouth' release - 'The Most Amazing Golf Shot Ever.'

The story provides a modern take on 'Practice makes perfect.'

Book Six
Undercover Cop
Find out how Dad became the centre of a criminal investigation, while working in a city shop in the latest book from the 'Words from Daddy's Mouth' series – 'Undercover Cop.'

The story also provides a modern take on 'Don't judge a book by its cover.'

Book Seven
The Dead Lawn Incident
Before Dad could become a lawnmower man, he had to get the lawn to survive – find out if he could in the latest instalment of the 'Words from Daddy's Mouth' series 'The Dead Lawn Incident.'

The story provides a modern take on the proverb 'You reap what you sow.'

Coming Soon   **Book Eight**
Crashing into a Police Car
Dad has ever only owned one car in his whole life, and it was never the same after 'Crashing into a Police Car' – the latest instalment from the 'Words from Daddy's Mouth' series.

The story provides a modern take on 'More haste, less speed.'

For Parents and Teachers

The Complete Guide to books 1 to 4 from the 'Words from Daddy's Mouth' Series
The team at Words from Daddy's Mouth have developed a notes and worksheets book that serves as a complementary kit for teachers, parents and tutors to assist with giving young readers a head start.

The book contains numerous practical tips, games and insights to learning techniques.

Enjoy easy access to the comprehensive and tailored reading collateral, with material for all of the first four books in the series conveniently consolidated in one place in this book titled - 'The Complete Guide to books 1 to 4 from the Words from Daddy's Mouth series.'

About how this all began (and why Lily Burgess is the author on the cover of the books)

By Matthew Burgess

Being a full time lawyer I needed a creative outlet, and in 2010, began writing business books for other professional service providers.

However there was still something missing. My wife said she married me because I made her laugh with the crazy stories I told her when we first met and that I should write a book.

Many years later we began to raise one, then two, then three and finally four precious girls and I started to share stories of my childhood with them.

It soon became one of our family's favourite pastimes listening to these stories about my childhood. Often embellished and seldom kept on track, the girls would be absorbed. What was fact became blurred in the magic of the stories told.

There is a strong undertone in these stories which carry various life lessons, while also ensuring a healthy dose of humour and role playing.

When my third daughter, Lily, was about four years old, she said, "Daddy, please tell me another story from your mouth."

From that day on, the stories became known as "Words from Daddy's mouth." It was therefore a natural progression that Lily Burgess would become the pseudonym for the authoring of my children books to help distinguish them from my other publications.

With so many stories, we had to create a list to remember them all (at last count the list was nearing 500). So over time a game developed where the girls would choose a number from the list. Whatever story related to the number chosen would be the story that I would tell.

Stories were usually told as the last part of the wind down of an evening, sitting together in a bedroom or on a lounge chair.

I hope you enjoy sharing the stories with your children.

Matthew (and Lily) Burgess

© 2014 Bambini Talent Group

www.ingramcontent.com/pod-product-compliance
Lightning Source LLC
LaVergne TN
LVHW020934090426
835512LV00020B/3361